Passive Affiliate Profits

Set and Forget Commissions with Passive Affiliate Promotions

by

Linda Tremer

ISBN: 9798631133686

CONTENTS

1	Passive Affiliate Profits	1
2	Finding the Right Products	3
3	What Have You Already Got?	9
4	Your Most Important Page	19
5	Passive Email Promotions	26
6	Passive Pinterest Promotions	30
7	Setting It All Up	32
	About the Author	36

CHAPTER 1
PASSIVE AFFILIATE PROFITS

Affiliate marketing is a wonderful way to make money in all kinds of niches and sectors. You can promote digital and physical products as well as services both high and low ticket.

But something affiliate marketers often overlook is *passive promotion*.

The kind where you set it and forget it leaving those affiliate commissions to keep rolling in.

Sounds great?

It is.

And yet so many people forget to do this or have simply never heard of passive affiliate promotion.

So, what is it?

Essentially it means adding your affiliate links to your content, pages, posts and other places where they can remain, continually earning for you.

Easy.

Except that you need to do this the right way, follow the rules (yes, there are some!) and maximize the impact of your passive affiliate promotions by knowing what and where works best.

Don't worry because you will learn exactly how to do that in Passive Affiliate Profits along with all my best tips and tricks for bringing in evergreen affiliate commissions for years to come.

Ah yes – that word 'evergreen.'

Which brings me on to the first and possibly the most important step in the whole process...

Choosing which products to promote.

So, let's dive right in there and discover how to select the kind of products that will keep raking in those commissions for you long after you've forgotten you ever put that link out there...

Trust me, I've done that many times. And it's a wonderful surprise when I look at my accounts and see an unexpected windfall from a product promo I barely remember or a steady stream of payments from a resource or tool I have recommended.

You can experience that thrill as well and it's far easier than you might think so let's get going and learn how you're going to find those products that will set you up for passive success.

CHAPTER 2
FINDING THE RIGHT PRODUCTS

When it comes to passive affiliate promotions, you want to think evergreen. It's no good promoting products that will disappear within a few weeks, leaving your links dead and your potential customers frustrated.

Instead, you need to select products and services with a good track record that will be around for the long term….as that means long term income for you!

More than that, you want to promote products and services that offer a clear outcome. It's the outcome that people really buy – the transformation that a product or service brings about in their own life.

Think about those muscle building or weight loss advertisements that show the Before and After. You can't get a much clearer outcome than that. Apply that analogy to products you are thinking of promoting and you won't go wrong.

If you don't understand exactly what a product or service can do for you within a few seconds, then your target audience won't understand either. There will be confusion rather than clarity with the result that they will click away.

I also apply the elevator pitch concept to something I am considering promoting. If you can't explain your fabulous idea to me in one or two sentences – or the time it takes for an elevator ride – then chances are I'm not buying and nor is anyone else.

Yes, I realize most people will teach you to start with the niche or the stats or what your target audience is chattering about on social media but I'm not most people.

All of those things are important but not as important as finding an offer that just about sells itself…

Because it's immediately and absolutely clear what it can do for you.

If you transpose that 'you' into 'your ideal customer' then you are on the right track. The track that leads to passive (as well as active) affiliate profits.

So where do you find those products?

The simple answer is: everywhere.

There are, of course, multiple platforms where you can find digital and physical products and services to promote as well as individual sites and affiliate programs. But the best kind of products to promote are the ones you are already using yourself or that you will obtain and then use before you ever think of promoting them as an affiliate.

There is simply nothing to beat an honest, authentic review or promotion of a product that you have put through its paces. And trust me, your audience can smell authenticity at a thousand paces.

Think about those 'reviews' you see all the time on the internet. It's patently obvious that the 'reviewer' has never even tried out the product or, at best, has glanced at a 'review copy.'

That's a world away from actually buying a product and going through not just the sales process but the actual process of using it and trying to make it work for you.

I always buy products in preference to getting a 'review copy' and that gives me the chance to experience that buying process from the exact same point of view as my target audience for promotions.

I have spent many hours attempting to make convoluted systems, methods and physical products work. I have also tried things out on my family as well as our pets (safely, of course!).

It's only by doing so that I can then decide if I want to promote the thing at all and, if I do, how best to convey that real experience to my audience with that clarity I talked about earlier.

Besides a clear outcome and doing what it says on the tin, I also want a potential passive affiliate promotion to have legs, i.e. I want it to be around for some time to come. Then I don't have broken links out there, annoying potential customers who might then think twice about following a recommendation of mine.

For that reason alone, I stick with a small stable of tried and tested products for my passive promotions that have built an excellent reputation over time and maintain that reputation.

I try to do the same with all my affiliate promotions although more active methods such as email broadcasts allow more scope when it comes to time restraints so I can, for example, promote something that's on a short term special if I think it's a really good deal for my subscribers.

With evergreen products, you can take the time to create a video demonstrating the product, for example. You can write up a review that shows your ongoing as well as immediate results using that product.

Demonstration is one of the best ways to promote a product as it instantly conveys credibility and proof, both of which your audience will appreciate. More than that, they are far more likely to act upon your recommendation.

There are some markets and niches that are forever evergreen, and I tend to stick within those as well as their sub-niches. The main evergreen markets are:

- **Health** – including niches like weight loss, fitness, mental health, stopping smoking and heart health

- **Wealth** – including niches like make money online, financial management, debt, mortgages and investment

- **Lifestyle** – including niches like personal development, self-improvement, passion-based hobbies, pets and DIY

  Romance – including dating, getting a lover back, mending a marriage, couples and dating coaching, senior dating and finding a husband/wife

Not all sub-niches are evergreen and not all products within niches are evergreen so make sure you check factors such as seasonality (not too many lawn mowers are sold in the depths of winter) as well as trends.

Trend-led products such as some – but not all – diet programs, fitness fads and, in particular, make money online 'systems' can have too short a virtual shelf life for you to consider promoting them passively as I teach you here.

Conversely, products that offer you recurring payments are perfect as these tend to be those indispensable things that people need enough to pay for an ongoing subscription.

This could be something like an autoresponder service or web hosting which are both excellent choices as people tend to stay with either of these for some time, not least because it's a hassle to migrate to another service.

Always think of that potential hassle factor. Think also of the 'can't live without' element. I, for example, subscribe monthly to several SAAS, or Software As A Service, packages that are essential to my business.

If I had bought one through your affiliate link, you would be looking at nice sums dropping into your account each month without you having to do any extra work.

In fact, setting up passive affiliate promotions takes very little work anyway. Especially when you consider the long term, ongoing results. It always amazes me that more affiliates don't do this. After all, it's as set it and forget it as you can get.

I can only assume they don't know how or they're too focused on those quick gains to be had from email blasts and hyped up scarcity.

Those promotions are all very well but do too many and you quickly burn your list. Far better to pick great products and promote them both actively and passively for immediate and ongoing, long term results.

So where do you find these products?

As I said, first take a look at what you are using already. Do you like your autoresponder, hosting and other services that you find indispensable? It's almost certain they have an affiliate program so join that and start promoting in the way I teach you in this course.

If you are working within another niche that fits those 'evergreen' criteria, again are there products you personally use? I work in the health niche because it is a passion of mine, specifically within fitness and even more specifically within yoga.

I know what yoga mat I prefer, which forms of yoga I like and the yoga courses on offer in my home city. All of these have affiliate programs in one form or another.

I know that at least one of my teachers offers a global coaching program via Skype. I can promote all of these with authenticity because of this and I also know that these are evergreen products that won't go out of fashion.

The same holds for the evergreen niches you may already work within or may be considering. If you're still looking for that evergreen niche, find one where there are plenty of products that people are willing to pay for that are preferably high and low ticket. Best of all, try to find ones that offer recurring payments.

As for finding affiliate programs, here Google really is your friend. If this is a product you use already then either look at the bottom of their home page for a link to their affiliate program, if they have one, or Google that product along with 'affiliate program.'

Do the same for products you don't yet use but remember what I said about trying something out properly first so you can recommend it with authenticity.

Or not.

Far better that you don't promote something you don't genuinely love even if it means missing out on potential commissions. Chances are that your promotions would not do as well anyway as your potential customers will be able to smell that lack of authenticity…just as you can.

Stay true to yourself, serve your audience as best you can by offering realistic, wholehearted recommendations and your passive affiliate promotions will serve up those ongoing payments for months and years to come.

Now that you know how to choose the right products, it's time you learned how to set up those passive affiliate campaigns. So, let's move on and learn exactly how to do that.

CHAPTER 3
WHAT DO YOU HAVE?

The first place to start with your passive affiliate campaigns is with your existing content.

Not only does this save you time and content creation, it also gives new life and earning potential to blog posts, videos, content upgrades and even eBooks that you might otherwise have simply forgotten.

Think about those pieces of content that fit with your chosen niche(s) and the evergreen affiliate products you have found using the criteria you have already learned.

Is there a blog post you already published on something to do with the niche?

Can you fit an affiliate link in to the existing content or tweak it slightly?

I find the best way to include an affiliate link is as a text-based one at the end of a piece in which I say something like:

"To learn more about the yoga method I prefer, take a look at this…"

With a link to a course, eBook or other product or service I have chosen to promote. I usually embed that link within the text, selecting text such as 'take a look at this' and then adding the URL to it so that it comes up as a clickable link.

This is very easy to do in WordPress and works better for me than more obvious promotional methods such as banners.

When it comes to videos, you may have a YouTube channel where you have already uploaded videos that relate to your niche or chosen product.

What you can do here is update the description to include your affiliate links but, as ever, make sure you comply with both YouTube's rules and requirements as well as those of the affiliate platform or program you are using.

Amazon, for example, are notoriously choosy about where you place links and hot on compliance. Take the time to read the affiliate terms and to follow them. Otherwise you risk not only losing your commissions but being permanently banned from the platform or program.

It is also essential that you include an affiliate disclaimer on your website. This tells your visitors that you may be earning a commission from affiliate links and it is best to check the law that governs your particular country or jurisdiction and to then include wording that complies with that law.

If you have existing content upgrades, eBooks and other suitable content where you could place an affiliate link then it is worth taking the time to do so. I generally do this in Word, where I create the initial document, then resave it as a PDF and re-upload to the appropriate place.

You can also place affiliate links on your existing download pages, thank you pages and anywhere that people access your content. Just make sure that you have that affiliate disclaimer in place.

Social media is somewhat different when it comes to older content as most algorithms favor new and fresh content, especially Pinterest. You are far better off adding affiliate links to your new Pins and posts, again ensuring that you comply with relevant rules and guidelines.

When it comes to your new content on your site and social media platforms, my advice is to plan your affiliate promotional strategy. I rarely if ever directly promote a product from a social media post.

Instead, I send people to a page or post on my site where I offer useful, valuable information related to the product and, of course, including a link to it.

Social media is all about engagement and conversation. People are not going to want to engage if you come across as too salesy or as if you are pitching to them all the time, simple as that.

Instead, you want to offer value in the form of a titbit of advice or information and expand on that advice or information in your post or page on your site.

I find that tutorials, demonstrations of how to do something and step by step processes are all highly popular content that will fit perfectly with many affiliate campaigns.

Don't forget that most people are in information gathering mode before they even think of buying something so give them that and then gently lead them towards the perfect solution for them with your affiliate link.

Cloaking Your Affiliate Links

A word here about cloaking your affiliate links which is advisable for a number of reasons. If you don't know what 'cloaking' means, it's the act of disguising a link so that your affiliate code is hidden within a link that is often shorter and neater than the often lengthy and untidy affiliate links with which you are provided.

There are several good WordPress plugins that disguise affiliate links and also allow you to track them.

Here is a selection of free ones:

1. **Pretty Links Lite**

   My cloaking plugin of choice as it's simple to use and yet effective. The lite version is free and perfectly **adequate for most needs.**

2. **Thirsty Affiliates**

   Thirsty Affiliates has more features than other free link-cloaking plugins although you have to pay for some of the add-ons. Again, the free version is fine for most users.

3. **WP Auto Affiliates**

   Uniquely, this free link cloaking plugin allows you to associate certain keywords with affiliate links and then automatically cloaks them for you as a link. Some users claim it quadruples your affiliate earnings.

So why use a link cloaking plugin at all?

First of all, it makes your link more appealing to visitors and less conspicuously salesy.

Secondly, it protects your affiliate commissions by obscuring your actual link which less scrupulous affiliates could otherwise exploit to steal your commissions, often by using malware.

Finally, cloaking your affiliate link means that it not only increases your click through rate, or CTR, but also deliverability of your emails if you are using affiliate links within those. Most cloaking systems allow you to track your clicks so you can keep an eye on your analytics and how well a promotion is performing.

Cloaking is also a good idea when it comes to your SEO, or search engine optimization as Google often penalizes sites with too many affiliate links or links that are too high up in content such as list-type blog posts.

For this reason, I advocate not just cloaking your links but sprinkling them through content sparingly. In a 1500-word blog post, for example, I might have 3 affiliate links spread throughout the content. In a shorter post, I would simply have one link at the end of the post.

It is also important to take other SEO considerations into account to ensure that your content is optimized and therefore will get as much organic reach as possible.

Some SEO tips include:

1. **Create longer blog posts**. Google loves extensive posts with 2500-3000 words often cited as optimal. Sounds a lot? Maybe but think about the impact that longer piece will have on your visitor numbers and therefore your potential sales.

2. **Find relevant longtail keywords using Google autocomplete and other keyword tools**. Simply start typing your search phrases into Google and it will serve up a host of other suggestions in the search box and in the related searches at the bottom of the page.

    You then drill down into those suggestions to find more and more relevant keyword phrases.

    Other keyword tools you can use include:

    -   Moz Keyword Explorer

    -   The Chrome extension Keywords Everywhere

    -   Answer The Public

All of which are free.

3. **Add graphics, infographics, tables and videos to your content.**
    All of these will help your SEO and user experience provided
    they are relevant and useful.

4. **Create great headlines, snippets, meta descriptions and titles.**
    Great headlines get your visitors reading your content while
    plugins like the deservedly hugely popular Yoast help you craft
    meta descriptions, tags and snippets for search.

Google's emphasis on user experience and the kind of content that provides it is no accident. This is also key to your success as an affiliate marketer so taking the time and trouble to craft optimized, compelling, valuable content that provides that all-important great user experience will also pay dividends in terms of your results.

In a digital world awash with content, yours needs to stand out if it is to compete. The best way to achieve that, aside from being relevant, valuable and optimized is to ensure that it is unique.

How do you do that?

By writing in your own voice and creating graphics, videos and other types of content that all reflect you and your original take on the topic, niche or sector.

Doing so will mean that your regular readers start to recognize your content immediately and will help to self-select your ideal audience.

Those who find your content resonates with them will be far more likely to act upon your recommendations and to buy while those who don't will simply click away to a site that is more in tune with them.

That is a good thing, believe it or not. You can't appeal to anyone and everyone and you don't want to. Instead, you want to build your own highly-committed tribe who will become repeat visitors and hopefully repeat buyers as well.

Supplying that tribe with the kind of content they love helps to build the all-important know, like and trust factor that leads to a sale. Or sales.

It also means that your passive promotions are far more likely to succeed as you know that the audience you attract with your content are also likely to enjoy and act upon it.

How do you know this? Because you also keep an eye on your analytics and see what posts do best. I like to use the free plugin Slimstat Analytics for this but there are plenty of other choices, including Google Analytics.

Installing a plugin like this on your WP site means that you can quickly and easily work out which is your best-performing content so you can serve up similar stuff to your eager audience. It's those popular posts that are prime territory for your passive affiliate links as they tend to have a long shelf life.

To maximize the impact of those posts, consider using a most popular posts plugin like:

https://wordpress.org/plugins/top-10/

Or create a separate page for your most popular content. You can either title this something like: 'Most Popular Posts' or use the approach I prefer and simply tell people to: Start Here. You will learn more about how to do this in the next module.

All too often, especially if you post regularly, your most popular content gets lost in the sea of new stuff so clearly indicating it and provided it in a curated section is not only another great way of serving your audience but it helps to draw them to that older content where you just happen to have placed your affiliate links.

Again, I must emphasize that you need to ensure those links are congruent with the content. Otherwise you will not only diminish their impact but also your authority in the eyes of your audience.

Never go for the quick or cheap sale with this approach. Instead, think long term and you will find that your results are commensurately long term in their rewards.

Your job is to build relationships through your content and social media posts. You do that with the quality of your content.

Another way to do that, of course, is through email marketing which is why I always recommend you have a lead capture form set up on your site so that your visitors can sign up or subscribe.

You'll find out more about how to utilize email marketing for passive affiliate promotions in the relevant module in this course. For now, make sure you have at the very least a simple autoresponder and lead capture forms set up.

When it comes to affiliate marketing, you really do need to look beyond the free systems which often have restrictions when it comes to marketing and instead invest in a robust provider who will help you grow your list and market to them, again over the long term.

Don't forget to use methods such as content upgrades alongside your giveaway report or ecourse or whatever enticement you use to get people to subscribe. Content upgrades can be as simple as a PDF encapsulating a long blog post into a handy downloadable that your visitor gets once they sign up for it.

All you need to do is create that PDF out of one or more of your popular blog posts – and certainly one that is long enough to warrant it – and then add a button or link so that your visitor can click to get it.

You could also create a cheat sheet, fuller report or white paper on a post, resource list or infographic that relates to the particular post.

The crucial detail is, of course, that you need to include your affiliate links in that content upgrade as well, bearing in mind everything I have taught you here about cloaking and relevancy.

Content upgrades are especially good for passive affiliate promotions as they tend to have an even higher perceived value than the initial post and are therefore digested with more attention. People tend to refer back to content upgrades which means they will also be exposed multiple times to your Calls to Action and affiliate links.

The beauty of all of these methods is that you only need to do them once and then forget about them provided you have followed my advice and selected evergreen products to promote.

Then your content can do the work for you while you get on with other things, safe in the knowledge that your passive affiliate promotions are perfectly primed to make you commissions on autopilot.

Let's move on and get even more specific now when it comes to certain pages on your site and the secrets I am about to share which will explode their value to you as a passive affiliate marketer...

CHAPTER 4
YOUR MOST IMPORTANT PAGE

Your website has several significant pages for an affiliate but there's one that is an absolute goldmine when it comes to passive affiliate promotions…

And it's not the About page as some people might tell you or your homepage as you might think…

It's a page you might not even have yet but you really need to create. A Resources or Tools page.

In fact, call it what you like but make it clear to your visitors that this is a helpful page full of the tools and resources you use to help you and your business.

Things like your hosting, your site builder or theme, your autoresponder, the social media scheduler you prefer, the graphics tool you can't live without….

The crucial part is that some or all of these should have an affiliate program you can join so that the links you provide to these resources are your affiliate links.

Equally as important is that you come across as genuinely helpful in your recommendations, which of course you are, as always. For that reason, I recommend you write a bit about how each tool helps you and in what way.

Make it personal and human. Offer the pros and cons but not in the way you often see of lists and bullet points.

Those always scream 'affiliate' to me. Instead, be anecdotal and mention how they help you and what you perhaps wish they did better but that those drawbacks are minor points. Don't spell out the pros and cons for each recommendation either. Vary it up, just as you would if you were providing a list like this to a friend.

In fact, that is my very best recommendation when it comes to creating a page like this.

Imagine you are talking to a friend who knows very little, if anything about internet marketing. They want to get started but have no idea where or how. You then suggest the best things you can think of to help them. That is the essence of your Tools or Resources page.

It's important not to overwhelm people with too many choices. Your job is to sift through the many autoresponder providers or hosting companies out there and recommend the one that you prefer, giving the reasons why.

Those reasons all too often include the fact that a particular provider pays the highest commission but, to my mind, that's a short-sighted approach.

If someone then acts on your recommendation and finds that the resource you suggest isn't that great after all, how do you think they're going to be about acting on your other recommendations? It also helps if they actually see you using the product you recommend.

So if I, say, have my site built using a particular page builder and then recommend it, people can see I walk my talk and also how well that page builder works.

If, on the other hand, I recommend a page builder or theme, but my site is built with something completely different, that's not exactly going to instill trust in my target audience. And quite rightly.

At first you may only have one or two things to recommend and that is absolutely fine. Your Resources or Tools page will grow with you. If it becomes very complex, it will help your readers if you divide it into categories such as, 'Email Marketing Tools,' and so on.

It can then become the basis for a great giveaway or content upgrade as people download the handy PDF version to keep on their own hard drive. Of course, you will include your affiliate links in that PDF version as well.

Don't forget you can also include book recommendations that relate to your particular niche and monetize those via Amazon.

These can be physical or Kindle books and can simply be books you have read and enjoyed, for example books on mindset or motivational topics, as well as those that are directly helpful or instructional.

Some people also like to include links to helpful courses on their Resource pages.

Again, if you do this make sure you include some non-affiliate links and links to free courses otherwise it will begin to look and feel like a promo fest rather than a helpful library of tools and recommendations, which is what it should be.

What About Your Homepage?

You will see affiliate links and banners on the homepage of many websites. After all, that's the first place most visitors land and therefore prime real estate for your promotions…

Or is it?

Thank about it for a second – how do you feel when you land on a homepage for the first time and see a whole bunch of banner ads, text ads and other obvious promotions?

Do you think that this will be a site focused on you and your needs?

Or do you do what I do and instantly assume that the site owner is more interested in what they can get out of you than what they can give?

It's an absolute truism in today's online world that you need to give before you receive. Imagine that you are meeting someone for the first time in a bar. All they do is talk about themselves and try to sell you on how marvelous they are. Do you warm to them?

Conversely, you meet someone who seems genuinely interested in you. They ask you questions about yourself, listen and respond to the answers and perhaps even offer some thoughtful insights that chime with yours.

Of those two people, which one is more likely to become a friend or even an acquaintance?

I think most people would prefer the second and that's because we all need to feel as if we matter. Greeting someone with helpful, educational, entertaining information that you think will resonate with them is the equivalent of meeting the second person.

Shoving a bunch of blaring ads at them is – you guessed it – the online version of the first.

Nobody likes to feel sold to. Everybody likes to feel understood. Your homepage is where you deliver your first impression. I believe it is therefore not the right place for affiliate promotions.

You have far better places to position those on your website, including individual posts and pages that focus on a topic relating to the promotion, that Resource page we just talked about and your Thank You pages after people have subscribed.

The Profitable Page You Probably Haven't Thought Of…

There is another page that has some crossover with the pages I have already mentioned, and which can also be highly profitable, sometimes even more profitable than a Resources page depending on your audience.

That page is a page you can call something like Start Here or Get Started and it works particularly well on sites dedicated to teaching or explaining more about topics that take the target audience from novice to intermediate or expert status.

Here's a selection of niches that include those topics:

- Internet or Digital Marketing
- Technical or Design Skills
- Writing and Self-Publishing
- Weight Loss or Fitness Methods or Regimens
- Arts and Crafts

The reason these pages work so well is that a complete novice usually arrives at your site in a state of some confusion.

Even someone with a degree of knowledge wants to be signposted through what you have to teach them and directed in a way that benefits them the most.

To help them do that you can supply them with links to the posts on your site that take them in, if possible, a logical order through the very first steps they should take and then on towards the more intermediate or advanced stuff.

If there is no obvious logical order, you can simply supply links to the posts which best reflect you and what you have to offer them about the topic or niche, or which have gained the most views and shares from your target audience.

I have seen self-help sites, for example, do this particularly effectively with links to their most loved posts or to the posts that may cover particularly sensitive topics.

The trick, of course, is to make sure that you choose posts in which you can also sprinkle your affiliate links, if you have not done so already, or create some which are especially suitable for those links.

You can re-use some of the links from your Resources or Tools page along with posts that don't have any links so that, again, this does not come across as one long continual sales pitch.

You are always aiming to achieve a balance between valuable information and entertainment for your audience along with links to products and services that you feel enhance or expand upon the information you have provided.

Remember that you are performing a service for your audience in curating content that they will most enjoy from your site along with products you have already curated from the hundreds or thousands out there to be the best solutions for them.

Always offer just one solution per blog post and preferably per problem or situation throughout your blog. That way, you don't confuse your audience while also maintaining your position as a trusted authority.

Yet Another Profitable Page

You may also have Thank You pages on your blog for your opt-ins and these are also an excellent place to offer your best recommendation to your new subscriber if you don't have a product of your own to offer here.

Again, present this as a helpful solution and include a text link rather than a big, blaring banner. You could add text along these lines:

'Thank you so much for confirming your subscription to receive my 10 Best Email Marketing Secrets. You can download your copy by clicking on the link below. I especially recommend Tip #4 which you can find on pg. 3 which shares the tool I use every day to get 100s more subscribers…and if you simply can't wait to get there, click here.'

You would then have a link to something like an autoresponder and I like to make sure it offers a free trial so that it underlines how I am trying to be helpful rather than sell.

If you can ask the vendor for a special deal for your subscribers, then so much the better.

Never be afraid to do this, even if you are new to your niche or to internet marketing in general. Vendors are there to sell their products and will be only too happy to offer a deal if you can demonstrate you can get them quality leads or sales.

CHAPTER 5
PASSIVE EMAIL PROMOTIONS

Yes, I know I said you wouldn't have to send out email after email to bring in those affiliate commissions...

And you won't.

Instead, you will create an autoresponder sequence or sequences once and then leave it to work its magic for you month after month.

Almost all autoresponder services offer you the ability to set up a sequence that gets mailed automatically to new subscribers or to people who have signed up to a particular list.

You set the first email to go out when you want, typically immediately or one day after someone has subscribed or performed another action.

You then set the follow-up emails to go out at set intervals on autopilot.

I typically set the first email to go out immediately and in this not only welcome my new subscriber but offer a valuable tip or other information that will be of immediate benefit.

This allows them to not only feel valuable and acknowledged but that I am immediately offering value in return. Not just any old value either but something they can act upon that will give them a quick, tangible result.

You could, for example, offer a tip that allows them to automate something that usually takes time or is tedious or you could break down what is usually a complicated step and give them your way of doing it quicker and easier.

This doesn't have to be anything amazing. We all have productivity hacks and tips that we like to use, or you can Google them for your particular niche if necessary.

You can also link to your Resources or Start Here page and suggest a particular resource or series of steps. This has the added benefit of exposing your subscriber to more than one of your affiliate links while still positioning you as someone super helpful.

I suggest you set up at the very least a 7-day sequence at first, sending out emails at one- or two-day intervals, all of them containing helpful information that relates to the reason they signed up in the first place.

If it was for a particular giveaway then expand on or illustrate the information in that giveaway report or whatever with your tips.

Congruency is so important when it comes to your autoresponder sequences. Someone who signed up for a giveaway video series on yoga is not necessarily going to appreciate a series of tips on muscle building, for example.

Once set up, your autoresponder sequences will carry on doing their job for you for as long as you wish. Here are two of the most popular autoresponders:

GetResponse http://www.getresponse.com/index/ltremer

Aweber - http://aweber.com/?473608

You can send out bonus lessons, a short email course.

You can send out tips that expand on the information in the course, related information on your site and other helpful follow-up emails.

You could then link back to the relevant post on your site rather than sending your subscriber straight to a sales page for an affiliate promotion you are running.

One thing I often do is send out just one great tip and include a link to a blog post on my site where there are other relevant tips including the one I have sent. This kind of post can simply build trust and engagement, or you could include an affiliate link if relevant at the end of the post.

Another great thing to do with your autoresponder sequences is to use story. People love stories and you can either tell them from personal experience or use a story that relates to your niche or topic, again to give the reader some kind of valuable or interesting takeaway.

One type of story that works especially well is one where you relate some kind of struggle or difficulty you have overcome that relates to your niche or topic.

This works on several levels. It shows you as all too human which makes you more relatable. It also teaches your reader something through your story and it is compelling because we all love to hear stories of someone else winning through against the odds.

You could also tell a story of one of your customers or students who has achieved a success or a win. This again teaches your subscriber something, especially if you focus on how they did that and how your subscriber could replicate that success.

At the same time, this kind of story underlines you as an expert or authority as well as someone they should pay attention to and whose advice they should follow.

Story helps to build connections and engagement which is hugely important when it comes to successful affiliate promotions.

As I have already said, people buy from those they feel that they know, like and trust. Story is a great way to get them to feel as if they know you a little better, especially if it is one that comes from personal experience.

And on that personal note, here's my best tip of all when it comes to your emails or, indeed, any and all of your copy: always write as if you are writing to one person. Preferably your ideal customer or target audience that you have already identified.

If you have not yet identified your ideal customer or target audience, ado this now. It will also help with your blog posts and all your content as it will help you create it with your ideal customer or target audience firmly in mind so that it resonates with them.

In the case of your emails, think of that one person as a friend. You wouldn't send a friend an email or bunch of emails laden with graphics and fancy links so don't do that with your autoresponder sequences.

Instead, stick to text and keep your tone informal and friendly. Remember that you want the recipient of your emails to think of you as a friend too.

Keeping your emails simple means that your reader can pay attention to your words and especially your calls to action inviting them to click on a certain link to, say, visit your Resources page. It is also makes your emails more likely to be delivered and therefore to be read in the first place.

CHAPTER 6
PASSIVE PINTEREST PROMOTIONS

Pinterest is a great passive promotional method.

Why passive? Because once you have created a Pin, the life of it is far longer than, say, a Facebook post with the average being three months. Granted that is not as long as some blog posts but still long enough to be worth doing if you are an affiliate marketer.

As with most promotional methods I teach you here, I recommend that you link from your Pin back to a post on your site. This also means that if you need to update an affiliate link, it's far easier to do so on a blog post to which a number of different Pins link.

I always suggest that you create more than one Pin for each affiliate promotion as different images resonate with, and appeal to, different people. You also need to take into account the Pinterest audience which is still largely female although this balance is slowly changing.

The wonderful thing about Pinterest is that creating Pins is free and they can drive an incredible amount of traffic to your blog.

For that reason, I also suggest creating Pins for your Resource and Getting Started Pages as well as borrowing a suggestion from the email marketing section in this course and including one tip on a Pin that sends people to yet more tips on a particular page on your site.

Don't forget that you can also send people to an opt-in page where they not only subscribe but are exposed to your Thank You page which you have, of course, set up as I suggested earlier.

In this way, your passive promotional strategies are holistic and reinforce one another. Always think like this when planning marketing campaigns, especially passive ones, as it means they will have far more impact than taking a scattergun approach.

CHAPTER 7
SETTING IT ALL UP

Here's the exciting part – you get to set up your passive affiliate promotions using all the knowledge you have gained in this course.

I suggest you start with one product, preferably the one that converts best for you, and add links for it to your existing content and, of course, your new content moving forward.

The reason I suggest you start with one is so that you can practice identifying the appropriate content and places to put your links which will help you become familiar with this process.

Then create your Resource and Start Here pages – or whatever you're calling them – so you can add the links there too as well as additional product links. If you have these pages already, so much the better.

You may want also to add your links to your Thank You pages and to content such as reports and eBooks that you sell or give away.

Doing this one product at a time helps you to get a good overview of everything you have in terms of existing content and material so that you can also see where you might place the next lot of product links. It also means you won't get confused between promotions.

I like to keep a record of where I have put my links and what I am promoting so that I can quickly update them across the board if necessary. I also like to track those links to see which are converting best and to tweak if necessary.

You can easily create a spreadsheet to do this and it is well worth the time it takes to do so because, again, once you've done it you simply add information as you create new promotions or update existing ones.

You can track links by adding tracking code when cloaking your links using most of the free plugins I have suggested. And, of course, updating your affiliate links is also quick and simple using a cloaking plugin so another compelling reason to use one.

Once you have set up your first product, move on to your next product, adding in those links in turn and so on until you have all your promotions set up. Depending on your niche, you may only have one or two products that you promote or twenty but remember to deliver value first however many you have.

By delivering value I mean creating content that solves problems for your target audience as well as entertaining and educating them. Blog posts and articles that provide solutions or tutorials as well as engaging opinions and useful information do far better than straightforward 'review' type posts.

I'm sure you have gone to Google a product review and been underwhelmed by what's out there, most of which is obviously simply an affiliate puff piece.

Your audience will be similarly skeptical which is why it is better for them and for you if, instead, you provide them with lively, informative, invaluable content that addresses all kinds of issues and topics arising in and around your niche rather than simply reviewing products within it.

I am not saying you cannot provide reviews – done properly they can also be invaluable for your readers. By 'properly,' I mean with enough objectivity and real information to help them make a buying decision. Or not. Your audience will thank you and be far more inclined to trust you if you not only try a product out first and report honestly on it but also say if you think it may not work for them or for certain groups of people.

If you do provide reviews, create a category on your site solely for them and always make sure you have that affiliate disclaimer in place. Also make sure that you follow the terms and conditions of individual affiliate programs and platforms, especially Amazon who set out very clearly where you may and may not place their links.

For this reason alone, it is wise to always send people to a post or page on your site rather than straight to a sales page. Another excellent reason is that you want to try and capture their email at your site, preferably by offering them some kind of giveaway or upgrade that also contains your affiliate links or takes them to a Thank You page where you have an offer intelligently placed for them to consider.

And that's really the art to passive affiliate marketing – doing it intelligently by respecting the intelligence of your audience.

People are not stupid. They come to your site because they want information or a solution or to be entertained or educated in some way. In living up to that promise, you can then offer them even more value in the form of products and services that you genuinely feel may help or be of benefit to them.

Set up your passive affiliate promotions to reflect this ethos using the steps you have been given here and you will not only gain customers but also a loyal list of repeat customers who buy everything you recommend because they have learned to like and trust you through the ongoing value with which you supply them.

That value also translates for you into excellent commissions if you do this correctly. Of course, I cannot promise what you will earn – that is up to you and the action you take.

But there are many affiliate marketers out there who earn passive 6 figure sums each year using exactly the methods I have taught you here. And keep pulling in those figures because these methods are evergreen.

The sooner you get started, the sooner you can do the same. I wish you every success with your promotions and I absolutely know that you can succeed. Simply keep this course close at hand to refer back to if you need to refresh your mind over a particular step or module and to follow when necessary.

Those steps are simple, and this is not rocket science. Follow them with the right attitude – the attitude I have taught you here – and you will be richly rewarded.

Check out this free book on affiliate marketing.

https://www.lindaanddean.com/lt-free-book

Would you like a course on how to create your own eBook? Check this out. https://www.easypdfformula.com/

Subscribe to my YouTube channel:

http://www.youtube.com/c/LindaTremer

Check out my blog:

https://lindatremer.com

And this great news magazine blog:

https://theinsidesecrets.com

with its YouTube channel "inside secrets" to give you tips and information on health, finance and lifestyle :
https://www.youtube.com/channel/UCEb8u0VdfmsWdhILi0AzFiw

ABOUT THE AUTHOR

My name is Linda Tremer and I am an Internet Marketer.

When I retired, I found that I could use a little bit of extra income (couldn't we all?). However, when I first started Internet marketing I was overwhelmed with the whole process. The hardest part was knowing where to start.

I finally learned how to make money online.

My goal is to help you find your way to making a full-time income online.